597.8 Pye

Why Am I an Amphibian?

Greg Pyers

Raintree

Chicago, Illinois

For information, address the publisher:
Raintree, 100 N. LaSalle, Suite 1200, Chicago, IL 60602

Typeset in 21/30 pt Goudy Sans Book
Printed and bound in China by South China
Printing Company Ltd

10 09 08 07 06
10 9 8 7 6 5 4 3 2 1

Library of Congress Cataloging-in-Publication Data
Pyers, Greg.
  Why am I an amphibian? / Greg Pyers.
    p. cm. -- (Classifying animals)
  Includes bibliographical references.
  ISBN 1-4109-2018-6 (library binding-hardcover) --
  ISBN 1-4109-2025-9 (pbk.)
  1. Amphibians--Juvenile literature. I. Title.
  QL644.2.P95 2006
  597.8--dc22
                              2005012219

Acknowledgments
The author and publishers are grateful to the following for permission to reproduce copyright material: APL/Corbis/© Joe McDonald: p. **6**, /© David A. Northcott: p. **15**; Basco/gtphoto: p. **21**; Bradleyireland.com: p. **9**; Tobias Eisenberg/imagequestmarine.com, pp: **12, 25**; Getty Images/Image Bank, p. **14**, /Taxi: p. **17**; Francois Gohier: p. **18**, /Ardea London Ltd.: p. **19**; © Brian Kenney: p. **24**; Alfredo Maiquez/Lonely Planet Images: p. **8**; Photolibrary.com: p. **13**, /Peter Solness: p. **4**,/ Animals Animals: pp. **7, 23, 26–7**, /SPL, pp. **10, 22**; Brian Rogers/Natural Visions: p. **16**; Dennis Sheridan/© David Liebman Nature Stock: p. **20**.

Cover photograph of a red-eyed tree frog reproduced with permission of APL/Corbis/© Joe McDonald.

Every effort has been made to contact copyright holders of any material reproduced in this book. Any omissions will be rectified in subsequent printings if notice is given to the publisher.

The paper used to print this book comes from sustainable resources.

Contents

Words that are printed in bold, **like this**, are explained in the glossary on page 31.

All Kinds of Animals

There are millions of different kinds of animals. There are animals that have four legs, animals that have more than 50 legs, and animals that have no legs at all! There are animals that are long and thin, animals that are round and wide, and animals that can change their shape.

But have you noticed that, despite all these differences, some animals are still rather similar to one another?

A toad has four legs and a round, wide body.

Sorting

In a carpentry shop, tools are sorted on different hooks so that the carpenter can find the right one. Animals that are similar to one another can also be sorted into groups. Sorting animals into groups helps us learn about them. This sorting is called **classification**.

This chart shows one way that we can sort animals into groups. Vertebrates are animals with backbones. Invertebrates are animals without backbones. Amphibians are vertebrates.

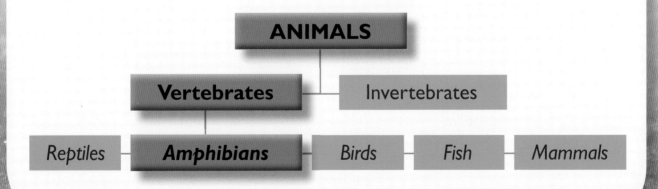

A Frog Is an Amphibian

Amphibians are one group of animals. There are about 5,740 **species**, or kinds, of amphibians. Frogs, salamanders, newts, and toads are amphibians. But lizards, otters, and seals are not. So, what makes an amphibian an amphibian? In this book, we will look closely at one amphibian, the red-eyed tree frog, to find out.

As you read through this book, you will see a ✔ next to important information that tells you what makes an amphibian an amphibian.

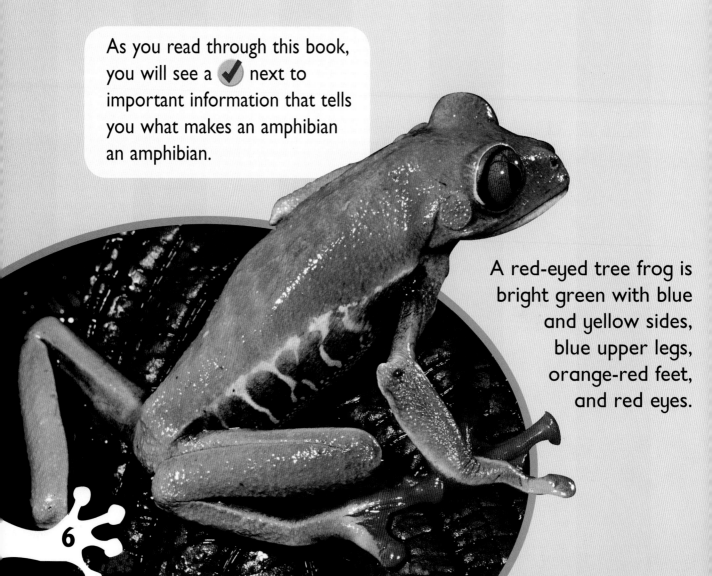

A red-eyed tree frog is bright green with blue and yellow sides, blue upper legs, orange-red feet, and red eyes.

Different frogs

Frogs are amphibians that have no tails. There are 4,740 species of frogs in the world. They live in many different places, called **habitats**. Many frogs live in **wetland** habitats, such as creeks and lakes. Some frogs live in deserts. The red-eyed tree frog lives in the rainforest of Central and South America.

Wet places

Amphibians are usually found in damp or wet places. Most amphibians prefer fresh water.

Tiger salamanders are often found in or near salty water in North America.

A Frog's Body

Like all frogs, the red-eyed tree frog has a short, wide body. Other amphibians, such as newts, have long, thin bodies. Like most amphibians, the red-eyed tree frog has four legs. The red-eyed tree frog's back legs are very long. Long legs help this frog to climb. All tree frogs have sticky pads on their toes for gripping leaves and stems.

FAST FACT

Some amphibians, called caecilians (say "suh-silly-ans"), have no legs. These amphibians look like worms.

A red-eyed tree frog's toes work like suction cups.

Skin

The red-eyed tree frog has soft, moist skin. Toads are the only amphibians that have dry skin. ✔ Like all amphibians, a red-eyed tree frog has no hairs, feathers, or **scales** on its skin.

Many amphibians have skin that can taste horrible to a **predator**. The red-eyed tree frog's bright colors warn predators that it would not be tasty to eat. Many frogs and toads actually have poisonous skin. The cane toad has poison **glands** near its ears. A predator that eats a cane toad can be killed by this amphibian's poison.

A red-eyed tree frog can change the color of its skin to help it hide from predators.

Inside a Frog

Inside a red-eyed tree frog is a skeleton of bones, including a backbone. The backbone is actually made up of many small bones joined together.
✔ All amphibians have a skeleton and a backbone inside their body.

Body temperature

✔ Like all amphibians, a red-eyed tree frog's body is the same **temperature** as the air or water around it. Frogs that live in cool **habitats** usually have cool bodies. The red-eyed tree frog lives in a warm habitat, so its body is usually warm.

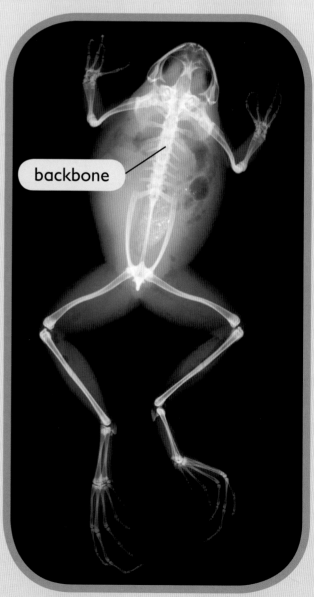

backbone

This X-ray picture shows the skeleton inside a frog's body.

Organs

There are **organs** inside a red-eyed tree frog. These include a heart, a liver, a stomach, and **lungs**. These organs all have important jobs to do.

Breathing

A red-eyed tree frog's lungs take in **oxygen** from the air. When a red-eyed tree frog breathes through its nostrils, air moves into its lungs. From there, oxygen passes into the blood. ✔ Like other amphibians, red-eyed tree frogs can also take in oxygen through their skin.

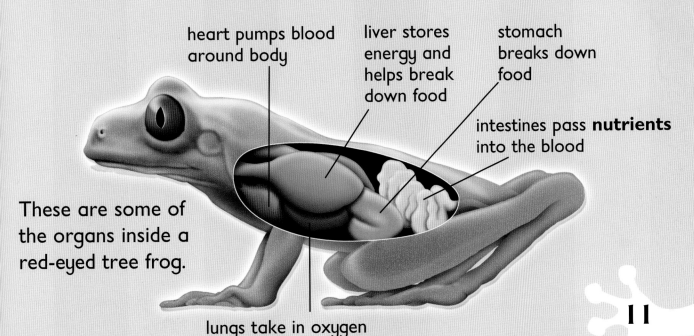

heart pumps blood around body

liver stores energy and helps break down food

stomach breaks down food

intestines pass **nutrients** into the blood

These are some of the organs inside a red-eyed tree frog.

lungs take in oxygen

11

Food

Red-eyed tree frogs are carnivorous. This means that they eat other animals. These other animals are the red-eyed tree frog's **prey**. When the frogs are small, their prey includes tiny insects, such as fruit flies. When they are fully grown, red-eyed tree frogs eat larger insects, such as grasshoppers. Sometimes they even eat other frogs.

A red-eyed tree frog pulls an insect into its mouth.

Hunting

A red-eyed tree frog hunts at night. It waits quietly on a branch. When an insect comes near, the frog shoots its tongue out at it. The tongue moves fast and its tip sticks to the insect. The frog then pulls its prey into its mouth. Some frogs do not have tongues. These frogs hunt for their prey under water.

Eating

A red-eyed tree frog swallows its food whole. It uses the teeth on the top of its mouth to grip its prey and keep it from escaping.

A red-eyed tree frog's eyes push down to help it swallow its food.

Senses

Like all amphibians, a red-eyed tree frog has senses to let it know what is going on around it.

Seeing and hearing

A red-eyed tree frog's large eyes give it an excellent sense of sight. Large eyes help the frog to see **prey** move in the darkness. A red-eyed tree frog has two ears, one on each side of its head. With these, the frog can hear other frogs calling.

A red-eyed tree frog's eyes give it a good all-around view.

Taste and smell

A red-eyed tree frog has taste buds on its tongue. If the tongue strikes prey that has a horrible taste, the frog will let it go. The red-eyed tree frog also has a sense of smell. It can use this sense to tell whether or not food is safe to eat.

Touch

You may have noticed that if you touch a frog, it will jump away. This shows that frogs have a good sense of touch.

A red-eyed tree frog smells with its nostrils.

nostril

15

Mating

In the rainy season, between October and March, male and female red-eyed tree frogs come together to **mate**.

Calling

At mating time, male red-eyed tree frogs begin calling from leaves low down in the rainforest. The males are calling female red-eyed tree frogs to come to them. They make a loud sound in their throats. The sound is kind of like a baby's rattle.

The sac under the male red-eyed tree frog's mouth fills with air as he calls. This makes the sound loud.

sac

Attracting a mate

Most male frogs and toads make sounds to attract females or to make females come to them. Different **species** make different sounds so that females know which male is which.

Getting ready to lay

When a female red-eyed tree frog reaches a male, the male climbs onto her back and holds on tight. The female holds onto the underside of a leaf with her sticky toe pads. Now, she is ready to lay her eggs.

The male red-eyed tree frog is smaller than the female.

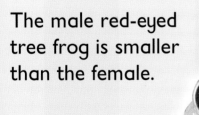

17

Eggs

The eggs come out of the female red-eyed tree frog's **cloaca** (say "cloh-acka"), which is an opening in her bottom. It may take a day for the female to lay 50 eggs. The eggs stick to a leaf. ✓ Like all amphibian eggs, the red-eyed tree frog's eggs have no shell. This means that the eggs must stay moist, or they will dry out and die.

FAST FACT

Female poison-arrow frogs lay some eggs that tadpoles will hatch from as well as some eggs for these tadpoles to eat.

Red-eyed tree frog eggs have a jelly coating that keeps them moist.

Growing

As the female red-eyed tree frog lays her eggs, the male **fertilizes** them. An **embryo** begins to grow inside each egg. Each embryo will become a tadpole (see page 20).

Most **species** of frogs lay their eggs in water. But the female gastric-brooding frog swallows her eggs after the male has fertilized them. The embryos grow inside her stomach.

You can see red-eyed tree frog embryos growing inside the eggs.

Tadpoles

When a pair of red-eyed tree frogs **mate**, the female lays the eggs on a leaf that is hanging over water. All amphibians hatch from eggs. Red-eyed tree frog eggs hatch five days after they are laid. A tadpole, not a frog, comes out of each egg. The tadpoles fall into the water.

A tadpole is the first stage in a red-eyed tree frog's life. Only later will the tadpole become a frog.

All frogs begin their lives as tadpoles.

Two stages

✅ All amphibians have two stages in their lives. They have a **larva** stage and an **adult** stage. In frogs, the tadpole is the larva stage. The frog is the adult stage. Tadpoles are very different from frogs. They have **gills** for getting **oxygen** under water. Frogs have **lungs** that they use for breathing oxygen from the air.

FAST FACT

The word *amphibian* comes from two words: *amphi*, which means "both," and *bios*, which means "life." So, an amphibian is an animal that has an underwater life, which is usually followed by a life on land.

An adult red-eyed tree frog breathes air through its nostrils.

nostrils

The Life of a Tadpole

Tadpoles must live in water because they have **gills** instead of **lungs**. Without lungs, they cannot breathe air.

Food

Red-eyed tree frog tadpoles find food near the surface of the water. They eat algae, which are simple plants. They also eat tiny animals, such as the **larvae** of **aquatic insects**, and dead animals.

FAST FACT

Tadpoles of the turtle frog of Australia do not swim. Instead, they stay in their eggs until they become frogs.

These animals are mosquito larvae, or mosquito young. Red-eyed tree frog tadpoles eat mosquito larvae.

Dangers

Red-eyed tree frog tadpoles have many **predators**.
These are animals that kill and eat them. Birds and fish
eat many red-eyed tree frog tadpoles. Of all the tadpoles
that hatch from their eggs, only a few will survive long
enough to become frogs.

A heron hunts for red-eyed tree frog tadpoles to eat.

Becoming an Adult

The tadpoles become **adult** red-eyed tree frogs 75 to 80 days after hatching from their eggs. The process of turning from a tadpole into an adult frog is called **metamorphosis** (say "metta-morf-a-siss"). ✔ To become adults, all amphibians go through metamorphosis.

Changes in metamorphosis

As the red-eyed tree frog tadpole gets ready to change into a frog, two back legs begin to grow. Front legs grow two weeks later. The tadpole loses its **gills**. **Lungs** grow inside the tadpole's body.

With no gills, the tadpole (below, at this point called a froglet) cannot get **oxygen** from the water. It must breathe air.

FAST FACT

Some salamanders may keep their gills and stay in the **larva** stage for their entire lives. This means they never become adults. But they can still **mate**.

Leaving the water

The tadpole's head changes shape and its mouthparts are shed. There is a new mouth underneath. Now, it is a froglet with a tail. The froglet is a pale blue color. It leaves the water and moves into the damp grass or plants of the rainforest. Soon its tail disappears.

At last, the froglet becomes an adult red-eyed tree frog. It spends most of its time in the leaves alongside the pools and creeks of the rainforest. A red-eyed tree frog may live for five to eight years.

Red-eyed tree froglets' tails turn brown before they disappear.

Is It an Amphibian?

A red-eyed tree frog is an amphibian, because:

- ✓ It has a backbone
- ✓ It has two stages in its life: a **larva** stage with **gills**, then an **adult** stage with **lungs**
- ✓ Its body may be warm or cool, depending on its surroundings
- ✓ It hatches from an egg that has a very thin skin, instead of a shell
- ✓ It has no **scales**, hair, or feathers
- ✓ It can take in **oxygen** through its skin.

A red-eyed tree frog is an amphibian.

Test yourself: Mexican axolotls

Mexican axolotls (say "aks-uh-lottles") live in cold lakes high in the mountains. Their body **temperature** changes with the water temperature. They have gills, so they can get oxygen from the water. Their skin is smooth and slippery. Mexican axolotls have a backbone, four legs, and a long tail. If a Mexican axolotl is put into warm water, it will soon lose its gills, grow lungs, and begin living on land.

Is the Mexican axolotl an amphibian? You decide. (You will find the answer at the bottom of page 30.)

Mexican axolotls are also called Mexican walking fish, although they are not fish.

Animal Groups

This table shows the main features of the animals in each animal group.

Mammals	Birds	Reptiles
backbone	backbone	backbone
skeleton inside body	skeleton inside body	skeleton inside body
most have four limbs	four limbs	most have four limbs
breathe air with **lungs**	breathe air with lungs	breathe air with lungs
most have hair or fur	all have feathers	all have **scales**
most born live; three **species** hatch from eggs; females' bodies make milk to feed young	all hatch from eggs with hard shells	many hatch from eggs with leathery shells; many born live
steady, warm body **temperature**	steady, warm body temperature	changing body temperature

Fish	Amphibians	Insects
backbone	backbone	no backbone
skeleton inside body	skeleton inside body	exoskeleton outside body
most have fins	most have four limbs	six legs
all have **gills**	gills during first stage; **adults** breathe air with lungs	breathe air, but have no lungs
most have scales	no feathers, scales, or hair	many have some hair
most hatch from eggs; some born live	all hatch from eggs without shells	many hatch from eggs; many born live
changing body temperature	changing body temperature	changing body temperature

Find Out for Yourself

If there are **wetlands** in your local area, they are sure to have frogs living in them. The frogs may be hard to see, but you will know they are there when you hear their calls. Each **species** makes a different call. How many different calls can you hear?

For more information about frogs and other amphibians, you can read more books and look on the Internet.

More books to read

Harvey, Bev. *Amphibians*. Philadelphia: Chelsea House, 2002.

Kalman, Bobbie, and Jacqueline Langille. *What Is an Amphibian?* New York: Crabtree, 1999.

Savage, Stephen. *Amphibians: What's the Difference?* Chicago: Raintree, 2000.

Using the Internet

You can explore the Internet to find out more about amphibians. An adult can help you use a search engine. Type in a keyword such as *amphibians* or the name of a particular amphibian species.

Answer to "Test yourself" question:
A Mexican axolotl is an amphibian.

Glossary

adult grown-up

aquatic insects insects that live in water

classification sorting things into groups

cloaca opening in a female frog through which eggs are laid

embryo early stage in the growth of a tadpole inside its egg

fertilize make an embryo grow inside an egg

gills organs that take in oxygen under water

gland part of the body that makes a liquid, such as poison

habitat place where an animal lives

larva (more than one are called larvae) first stage in amphibian life. A tadpole is the larva of a frog.

lungs organs that take in air

mate come together to make new animals

metamorphosis when a tadpole changes into a frog

nutrient part of food that an animal needs to survive

organ part of an animal's body that has a certain task or tasks

oxygen gas that living things need to survive

predator animal that kills and eats other animals

prey animals that are eaten by other animals

scales hard plates that cover skin

species kind of animal

temperature how warm or cold something is

wetland lake, pond, stream, or swamp

31

Index